THE SOLO PARENT'S GUIDE TO MANAGING A HOUSEHOLD

THE SOLO PARENT'S GUIDE TO MANAGING A HOUSEHOLD

AVERY NIGHTINGALE

CONTENTS

CHAPTER 1

Introduction

The objective of this project is to provide a general description of who single mothers are and to present a "Taylor-made" guide providing assistance with household chores and any other single parenthood needs and duties. The increase in women's labor force participation in the United States and gaining education have changed the outlined picture of the single mother, which traditionally was believed to be a property of only females with lower income and education. Moreover, it has brought to attention the problem of demanding and sometimes unreasonable role of a mother in the society – an expectation of combining full-time job with an uncompromised care of one or more children. Even though it may result in mental or physical overstrain, single mothers take truckloads of sensitive attitude if they decide to share some of their responsibilities with the other parents – fathers, usually.

There's an old saying: "Necessity is the mother of invention." And that sums up the situation facing more than 12 million single parent families in the United States. In 2013, single mothers living with children younger than 18 years were about five times more likely to live in poverty than their married counterparts, while single mothers were six times more likely to be poor. As a result, single mothers may have to make tough decisions about how to divide their limited time, money, and emotional resources. In addition to traditionally feminine duties such as grocery shopping, cleaning, and cooking, single mothers who work outside the home have less time for childcare and leisure activities than those who are not employed.

CHAPTER 2

Financial Management

As a solo parent or having a single income provider in the family, means finding extra means to generate income or overtime pay. If a person is currently employed, having an extra job or earning extra will mean opening a family-owned business or exploring entrepreneurship. Opening a business can be an opportunity to tap into a large source of potential revenues and even commercial success. On the positive side, extra revenues can meet all the necessary expenses rather than merely relying on paid employment. Proper budgeting, therefore, in this case, remains to be a necessary step in managing our finances. With proper budgeting and investing, these revenues that one can have through new business ventures can supplement the regular revenues from paid employment.

The reality for most sole parent households is the financial capacity to meet the basic needs of the family, which involves having a stable income that covers regular expenses and has extra for unexpected situations. As a solo parent, financial capacity for the family is one of the most important factors that needs to be given emphasis. The person should be able to meet the daily needs of the family like food, commute, and even leisure to keep a balanced family life. Planning the family's budget not only includes daily expenses, it also needs to account for long-term goals such as saving for bills, tuition fees, and other investments including savings for emergencies.

CHAPTER 3

Time Management

2. Take care of necessary tasks as soon as you walk into the house. You may be really busy, and the household might be a mess, but take the kids in, then immediately do the things which absolutely need to be done. Need to feed the dog? Take care of this task as soon as you and/or the kids walk in through the door. Ideally, they should be given a snack or start on homework while you prepare dinner. Not having to worry about too many things needing to be taken care of immediately after getting home makes the afternoon/evening transition much smoother.

1. Assess what tasks need to be done daily, weekly, and monthly. This will help prevent becoming overwhelmed by tasks. For example, tasks that need to be done daily might include: dinner, getting kids fed, bathe and off to bed, dishes, sweeping, and providing clean clothes. Weekly tasks could include bill paying, grocery shopping, etc., and monthly might include bills; house maintenance such as painting, minuscule repairs, etc. Assess what needs to be done, how often, and then figure out realistically when you can adopt these projects.

Time management, particularly as it relates to households and living spaces, depends on each individual parent's schedule. As a working parent, one may have less time to tackle household responsibilities compared to a non-working single parent. Regardless, all solo parents can benefit from the following suggestions:

CHAPTER 4

Meal Planning and Cooking

A crockpot or Instapot are kitchen devices that solo parents swear by. They help to prepare hearty and delicious meals with minimal energy and time, which is why many people consider these kitchen devices as great tools for managing home life. Working parents in particular might want to make the most of these devices and get dinner ready at the touch of a button. There are many recipes online that you can try out and are definitely not limited to just stews and soups, which is the top reason why you need to have one available in your kitchen even as a solo parent. Whether it's for nights that you don't have enough cash on hand for take-out, or busy time at work, or when your family craves a home-cooked meal, having a homecooked dinner ready at the touch of a button is definitely a game-changer.

To pull away from take-out meals and eating outside, cooking with your children can be a life skill that you start practicing in the kitchen. Grocery runs might be challenging as well, which is why several solo parents order their groceries online or plan careful trips to the store. To save time, you can plan your groceries for the entire month or use a popular grocery delivery app to facilitate your convenience. Consider joining cooking preps with other solo parents and bond with your children on weekends. Preparing meals that can be frozen or quick meals that can be cooked after a long day is also an efficient method to manage your family's meal plan.

CHAPTER 5

Cleaning and Organization

I am not a personal fan of the mop I mentioned. I have tried so many mops and this is by far the best. It's a pleasant feeling to clean the floors and not stress; the floor is indeed quickly cleaned up without any issues. But the use of this mop as a main cleaning tool should not be overstressed; it can be helpful in getting grout and tile clean as well as in mopping floors. Our favorite implement for daily cleaning is the Swiffer pollosweep. Each pad lasts about two weeks and it's really easy to just sweep away the dust and cat hair around the main part of the apartment daily, leaving floors just that little bit cleaner. A mini teardown of the main living area once a week makes it easy to view houses that have been tidied and uncluttered as well, helping keep stress at bay and the floors clean.

Dirt, clutter, and debris can be problems in any household, but it's even harder for a single person to keep up with cleaning and organizing their living space than it is for a two-parent family. Getting kids to pick up after themselves is a good start, but there's still the regular maintenance of important but dull chores like cleaning the kitchen floor. There are several ways to make daily cleaning easier for the solo parent. First, giving up the idea of what Swiffer calls the perfect clean is the first step in solving the problem of a dirty floor or sticky stovetop, or streaked tile. One can find a DIY pole mop with cleaning pads attached to it and a dish soap dilution.

CHAPTER 6

Home Maintenance

Let's start with the fact that you really need to check every corner and part of your house just to see how your dwelling is holding up, especially if you are buying a new one. But for existing homeowners, maintaining a household is an important topic at hand. While you may replace electrical wiring, repaint your walls, fix your leaky toilet, there are still problems you can't just DIY away. For example, the older your sewage system is, the more susceptible it becomes to damages, not to mention blockages. Older sewage pipes were built using different materials which are prone to suffering from ground movements. Roots can sneak into your sewage pipes, preventing drainage and backing up water, sewage, and the like into your house. This is obviously a situation you want to avoid, so prevent it by having your sewage pipes checked and cleaned regularly.

When was the last time you had the electrical lines in your house checked? How about your water lines or gas lines? Do you know when you need to replace your roofing or when it is time to have your sewage system cleaned? Just the sound of these questions makes you want to dread home maintenance issues. While these sound troublesome, it does not take a lot of effort to prevent these issues from ever happening. But where do you start, you might ask. You unravel its potential to cause you problems by taking preventive measures such as conducting routine maintenance checks, repairs, upgrades, and you can even consider opting for comprehensive home warranties that cater to all crucial components that make up your home.

CHAPTER 7

Childcare and Education

Find the right school for your child, including if he shows signs of learning at a faster or slower pace than average. Despite the name, your neighborhood schools may not be the best for your children, even in this era of school choice. The advice on Greatschools.org, a website that says it rates 200,000 schools, may be remotely reliable. Schools with in-person themed or Capitol Hill Day School Dividend Days offer occasional evenings to parents. In Maryland, with 2007 income statements, residents with earned income in excess of $38,000 per year and eligible children can get a $2,000 maximum refundable credit. The national Head Start office reports that nearly 50 projects refine the offering of support to children and their families, including to parents in prison, who are also part of the teams who apply for assistance once release is near. This support includes visits when kids are in school and quarterly "secondary" visits when children are with their primary caregiving parents.

Whether you work outside of the home or not, you need a good childcare arrangement, and if your child is school-age, help for before- and after-school care. Stay-at-home parents also need options for a break from child care. Interview potential caregivers in person and, if possible, with your child. Even "permanent" nanny care may need backup options (such as private babysitters and drop-in care) because providers get sick and have to meet other personal obligations. Get resources and help: Families Make the Wheel Go Balance, 1-800-843-5437, reaches the National Parent Helpline network of state-based support resources, which will refer to storytelling venues and in-home service providers, among other resources. Local YMCAs, which offer parent-led indoor playtime (some allow drop-offs if the child is a member), after- and before-school programs, and occasional evening childcare, are another resource. Thirty-six states have parent home visiting programs.

CHAPTER 8

Self-Care and Well-being

Respect your feelings. It's human nature to feel weak, yet make certain the feeling will serve as an incentive to conduct more work vigorously, instead of not acting at all. As for this situation, it is best that you cultivate friendships and a communication network. There are so many different clubs and groups that consist of solo parents with a duplication of ups and downs that are willing to help each other in these times of crisis. By interacting with these people, you could know more about their daily accomplishments. You'll have more strength, enthusiasm, and inspiration to face the world. If you want all of the bonding, you could consider joining spiritual groups which offer communal assistance. Evidently, these groups offer continual moral fortification and inspiration. Remember, strength is might.

There would be times when you think that you are already in control of the circumstances and you are capable enough to survive the many trials of being a solo parent. You might feel tired and exhausted but still, at the back of your mind, you know you need to exert a little patience and willpower to supervise your child. But the law of nature tells us that our bodies and mind have limitations. You found yourself reacting violently from simple incidents whenever you feel hopeless and weak. This is the perfect time to give yourself a break. You need to pamper yourself, given the fact that you are the only one to do such a task. You need to find time to sleep your strains away. Rest is always the number one option whenever you're worn-out.

CHAPTER 9

Social Support and Networking

One resource that I discovered completely by accident was my new friend and neighbor in a new city—a kind and nurturing 70-year-old woman who officially entered my life as my baby's nanny, but speedily became like a grandmother to my kids, an esteemed mentor to me, an oust the negative voices of your kids' piece of parenting advice, and a good cup of hot chocolate, depending on the circumstance. She is good friends with dozens of elderly women just like her, and now I am the Mercedes-Benz, the V8 engine that purrs along those women's lives; my kids are the delightful music that drowns their boredom now and then. When the final project of my kids' homeschooling year included delivering bakery to a specific friend's coffee table, my kids had experienced one of the most beautiful days in my whole existence as a parent. When busy neighborhoods get together, the environment is joyfully rich.

A supportive community allows you to vent and get advice, to borrow a tool or an ingredient, to share a skill or rent a believed-unnecessary resource. Other single parents who are further along the path than you can share their wisdom to help make the path smoother for you. The give and take of social support in the most genuine form enriches your and your kids' daily lives—it makes your surroundings feel more social. Rediscovering community without the need to prove any given accomplishment is both humbling and comforting. Just buy your neighbor a jar of jam made from your kids' graduating paper route earnings and see how the love comes back in one form or another.

The most important tip for a solo parent is to have a support group. When times are tough, it helps to have a friend, a family member, or your own parents come over and help take care of the kids or the house chores. You'd be surprised at the number of friends and family willing to help you when something urgent or important needs to be done—ask with humility and you'll never know just how much you may be given. Venture out and discover these treasures of support in your community as well. From your place of worship or through a local social services group, you will likely meet other parents (at times single parents like yourself) who are compassionate souls.

CHAPTER 10

Balancing Work and Family Life

If your workplace offers you the flexibility to spread out 8 hours of work over 10 hours, take advantage of the benefit. Use that flexibility to change your hours depending on your and your kids' needs. An extra hour at home can mean the difference between leaving work at 5pm and leaving work at 6pm, which can be huge for kids who hate bedtime. Childcare isn't just a female problem. Daycares don't open on time for an 8am start (which is silly). Many men leave work early as it is. If there is a rush to leave work by 5pm because we have kids to pick up, many men will argue (fairly) that they have the same issue. Fostering an equal environment also helps promote having more women in our field. Consider asking those who do leave work early to come in by 7am so that they can make an attempt to share the childcare arrangements.

In my work as an industrial psychologist, I often get asked by coworkers and clients whom I consult for about how to balance the demands of home life with the demands of work. In our department, we are often called upon to work long hours. One underappreciated fact about my life is that I am the primary caretaker for two children. Here, I give some of my hard-earned wisdom. Keep in mind: YMMV.

CHAPTER 11

Managing Stress and Burnout

My whole "Let's help them learn about managing stress" mantra started when I recognized that even I only wanted to teach my kids "how to clean the house" so as not to be a messy, unmanageable burden. That was my response to feeling very much like I was a messy, unmanageable burden, with not one iota of me dedicated to seeking capability within myself beyond getting the kids into a structured, intrinsic routine. I wanted the kids to be able to take care of themselves, for no other reason than not being a burden to anyone else. This was going on in my head, whether they recognized it or not. They did recognize it, by the way, but not in the way that I was calculating and quite aware of. There's really no better way than hearing it from my kids to make me question my own parenting though, huh? There's more work to be done.

Raise your hand if you've heard this one before: "Never put off until tomorrow what you can do today." For those of us who've ever tried juggling a to-do list fit for a family of five with a baby strapped to our chest and a toddler clutching to our leg, this phrase can make us scream out loud. It's stressful to do it all. Many times, this phrase can feel like it was designed specifically to add insult to injury, to taunt the under-scheduled and ill-prepared. The not-so-average solo parent knows that the only way we're going to make it another day is to accept that our #unconventionalstyle is not going to let us jump through hoops and over fire-pits in order to survive. Sometimes, it's one step in front of the other. And other times, you just breathe. If you need to feel organized in order to keep breathing, here's your chance. If you believe learning ways to manage stress will help you find similarities in other solo parents that can bring a smile to your face, here are some takeaways. Positive or negative, never forget that our empowered-voice — dot, dash-dot — is an exclamation mark!

CHAPTER 12

Co-parenting Strategies

A ny assemblage of stakeholders who assumes responsibility for fostering the healthy growth and development of children can include family members, friends, neighbors, siblings, parents, or partners of the custodial parent who is primarily responsible for completing parenting duties. Divorced individuals who use the same strategy can benefit from each other's knowledge. Co-parenting is a method in which parents uphold a common vision and collaborate to improve the psychosocial, sexual, academic, emotional, and psychological development of children by harmoniously executing child-rearing duties. Successful co-parenting thus benefits kids, parents themselves, and society. Co-parenting consists of four basic functions: the provision of a secure base, communication regarding the progress of the kids, alliance and shared decision-making, and the equal contribution of funds necessary to raise a child.

Raising a child alone is difficult and time-consuming. Custodial parents who are solely responsible for the physical, emotional, and psychological well-being of their children frequently grow weary and exasperated from shouldering the plenitude of parenting duties on their own. Solo fathers and mothers need supportive networks to obtain resources and to identify the most effective parenting strategies. This article offers tangible advice and parental guidance to address the many challenges commonly experienced by solo parents, including: discipline, domestic chores, relationships, maternal self-esteem, stress, free time, and attention. The suggested techniques aim to decrease parenting stressors and increase disagreements and miscommunication between stakeholders. Custodial parents require considerable time and funds to fully support their family.

CHAPTER 13

Dealing with Emotions and Grief

There's no need to rush your grief as society sometimes dictates. It's alright to recognize that grief is an individual process. You can give yourself time and space to honor what you've lost. If you're having a challenging time letting yourself talk about it, look for an outlet by journaling, creating art, or speaking with clergy or a mental health professional. Finally, always remember to acknowledge and celebrate strengths and accomplishments as well as the milestones and achievements of old friends, new friends, and your village. Appreciate the love and support you give to your family members, and don't be reluctant in expressing your thanks for the village you've found and that embraces you just the way you are. You have rights, it's all right to honor them.

Begin by recognizing and acknowledging your feelings, then give yourself time to let them out. Cry when you feel like crying. Allow yourself to get angry and punch some pillows. Reach out to supportive people who will listen, not members of your support system who might gloss over your pain with well-intentioned clichés. Remember, there are some people who might not offer you support for the simple reason that they don't know what to say or how to act.

It doesn't mean they don't care. Though you might find it hard to believe, there will be people who genuinely want to help – it's just a matter of finding them. In the absence of these people, recognize that you can provide support for yourself in many ways. The simplest might be in avoiding triggers like familiar sounds, music, places, or familiar routes to and from work if possible.

CHAPTER 14

Establishing Routines and Boundaries

Establish a curfew (say 8:00 P.M. for the younger children) for the use of the telephone and all other noisy pursuits. Use relaxing music and tapes for a quiet atmosphere. The children can use this time to work on homework, read for pleasure, set up the table, or do minor chores. Talk to them during commercial time on TV. Be together while doing your projects.

1. Set a regular time frame for you to accept/return phone calls. 2. Set a regular time frame for meals. Plan multi-purpose meals many weeks in advance. These can be prepared quickly and do not entail additional purchases, preparation, or clean up. Cooking around a "theme" speeds up the process. 3. Have a month's or at least a week's grocery list prepared in advance. This way you can take advantage of food's cheaper "seasonal" prices and avoid impulse buying. 4. Assign days or blocks of time for cleaning, maintenance, special chores, etc. For example, Mondays: wash your car, clean out the fridge, cook a large enough batch of food for a week's lunches. The kids clean and maintain their rooms on a specific day.

Do your week's food shopping on the same day each week. Assign tasks to your children and do your household chores on the same day every week. When everyone knows what to expect, less time and energy are wasted on "bickering and nagging." The establishment of a routine also teaches the children to become self-disciplined and on-time adults. Established routines help you establish firm boundaries and teach children limits. They know, for example, that you do not answer the phone or accept visitors at certain times. Children who are trained in these routines are more cooperative and obedient and are reported to have a better self-image and greater freedom and social interaction than those who grow up without guidelines.

Managing Household Chores

Set a time to decompress with your kids after school. You could ask about their day as they wash their hands and have a snack or beverage. Making conversation will help ease the kids into the next task and get them to put things in their proper place. Once everyone is settled, resume your chore engagement process. Set regular assessments to share tasks that interfered with school work and speculate on reasons such tasks were not completed. This open discussion will help all of you generate traditions and routines that allow home and school life to run smoothly.

Delegate chores that require little supervision to your kids when you are busy. For example, the younger children can feed the pets while the older kids can chop, peel, or slice vegetables, make their beds, and take out the garbage. As you entertain younger children or work on complex tasks, involve the older ones in the kitchen. This gives them the opportunity to experiment with cooking but with the option to seek assistance from you when you concentrate on other things. They also get to ask questions and improve kitchen ethics every time they taste the meals they have just made.

To efficiently manage household chores without feeling overwhelmed, delegate simple tasks like folding napkins and cutting invisible threads hanging on garments. Share household chores that align with your kids' skill levels. This transforms simple tasks into meaningful projects that boost their confidence as well as lighten your load. Anticipate needs at regular intervals to create and maintain habits that support the chore management process. A quick scan of the environment will reveal tasks that require your full attention or those you can enlist your kids to help you with. Once you identify tasks you want to do later, make a note and set a reminder if the task cannot be completed immediately.

CHAPTER 16

Budgeting and Saving Money

Amy Dacyczyn's Tightwad Gazette books were my financial early education that I still return to often. Even though the books were published in a time before the internet, social media, and iPhones, most of her anecdotal data still rings true. Even fasting from marketing is still a heat-seeking missile for my depression-era mindset. Sunny and Christian have become close friends and we both go to each other's houses to repair or cook for one another. I see Christian's family as kindred spirits to my own. Uncompromising and resourceful. Amy keeps a notebook tracking what she and her son spend, extending their selves into a long-term conversation on where their priorities lie. It's heartwarming to see.

The most complicated thing about money is figuring out how much we think we're worth. And no matter how much we have, we all want more. Keeping your money in check is about knowing what's happening to it and putting your resources towards the things you value. If you value your time more than shopping for deals, then shopping at the closest store is worth the extra cost. If you value your kids' education above all, then putting money aside to ensure they avoid getting into debt when they get out of school is a worthwhile investment. A restriction on money is an excuse to get creative! There are lots of ways that kids can help out around the house to create value as they grow. Time saving is a big part of budgeting, especially with kids around. You should know that what is interesting or fun for them is most likely not a money saver. Laundry day at your house could look like a carnival sideshow!

CHAPTER 17

Creating a Support System

2. Manage expectations (yourself, your children, others). Managing your own expectations is very important. Always - always remind yourself not to overstretch and take on too much with no choice but to half-ass everything. Learn to accept and be okay with the fact that some things will not be done today - it's perfectly fine. This is so that when you are caring for your children and are unable to be home for dinner, entertain guests, or keep up with extracurricular activities, you are able to honestly explain why and have everyone accept the situation. Always give your children time to talk to you/help out - including you in any plans. I know kids have an uncanny knack of choosing the most inconvenient times to talk to you, but sometimes it's the only time they're free to do so. Involving them (obviously age-dependent) allows them to see and understand what's going on with you and the home front.

1. Create routines. Routines are an important part of your day-to-day management as not only do they provide structure, they also allow a sense of comfort and security for the children. With school (especially for younger ones who sometimes have half days), the routines involve a standard wake-up time, eating breakfast (for those

who barely have an appetite in the morning, it's important to make sure that good food is available at school, so perhaps offer them a snack before bedtime), dropping off/picking up, activities accompanying their respective days at school, playtime followed by dinner and bedtime. If they express discomfort with the new routine, just assure them that once they get used to it, it's going to be much smoother.

It is important to have a good support system. Some solo parents lean heavily on their immediate families, but it is best to establish a wider network (as it is also healthy for everyone to have some respite/ space from each other). Create a drop-off/pick-up network, a friend you can call on any time of day or night, and someone you can rely on to look after the children for school meetings and events, and you can do the same for them. Also, it is essential to network and get out into the wider world. The internet is a boon here - find groups and forums (some have actual meetups) where you can connect with other solo parents, as well as family events such as story time in bookshops, various groups attached to libraries or churches.

CHAPTER 18

Health and Safety in the Home

Here are the steps you need to follow since upholstery leather furniture cannot be cleaned using traditional furniture cleaner: 1. Use a slightly dampened cotton wool with clean water. 2. Wipe the affected area gently in a dabbing motion to avoid smearing. 3. Repeat the process until the region is dry and clean. 4. Ensure the surface is dried using a damp cloth. 5. Use a specialized wood cleaning product to remove crayon marks. 6. Use a dry, soft cloth to apply the wax as instructed by the cleaning product manufacturers. 7. Buff the waxed area gently when the application is dry.

In the healthcare field, you will find some generalized cleaning methods that can save you time, but they use unsafe substances that can be harmful to upholstery. Some stains like sauces, wine, ink, and chocolate could be favorites, and you can try homemade cleaners used for these types of stains that might work well for you. Do spot testing in unseen areas like under the sofa and patch them securely before applying to a larger area.

When upholstery looks or smells clean, it may not be. When cleaning your upholstery, ensure no solvent, preservative, toxic ingredients, or chemical contamination is left behind. Use natural ways to clean your fabric in a safer way, not just for the fabric, but for your children and plants. Stains can be tricky and can cause damage if not treated properly. Make sure you take care of stains correctly and do proper treatment.

CHAPTER 19

Encouraging Independence in Children

An example of this are the pre-teen boys in our village who find themselves on their own during the day sometimes, because their moms work. Luckily, we brought up these boys to act like little men, capable of cooking basic dishes, and completing household chores. They also carry themselves well when in public, and are respectful generally to adults. Depending on the family, they have variances as to interest in sports, academics and social acumen; however, the in-charge attitude is present in all the boys of this age-group. It's a pleasing thought that these boys are en route to manhood, and don't even realize it!

In our quest to raise independent kids, it's a good idea to allow them to solve problems without always having a parent intervene in cases where it is safe for them to do so. It's also beneficial to nudge them toward discovering their own voices and out of their safety zones, so that they will be able to interact with others effectively and come up with solutions to the challenges they encounter. The key is to provide a balance and make them empathetic to others' needs too.

How do you raise independent kids? It's a dilemma solo parents face as we try to strike a balance in making our kids overly dependent (clinging to us whenever they encounter obstacles) or on the other end of the continuum – raising adults who are overly independent (believing that they alone could solve problems, not reaching out for help or not involving the family in decision and problem-solving).

CHAPTER 20

Finding Reliable Childcare Options

There are many individuals who offer babysitting services. If you are planning to hire one, make sure to conduct multiple interviews and ask for recommendations from trusted friends. A babysitter can be a long-term solution if you require frequent child care. In case of emergencies or other commitments, grandparents, aunts, and uncles can also be a great source of child care. Additionally, enrolling your child in a daycare or preschool program can provide them with social interaction and education while you are at work. Some schools offer reduced rates for regular or routine care. If you are eligible, you can also consider applying for federal funds through the RCC program to help cover the costs of child care while you work or attend school.

Solo parenting can make it difficult to coordinate daily schedules with a reliable caregiver. A child may occasionally miss having both parents present. However, when both parents are busy employees with demanding jobs, scheduling can become a nightmare. Even if you have a partner or family member who can help occasionally, you may still need child care twice or three times a week. Hiring a babysitter can be expensive, with rates in Queensland sometimes exceeding $25 per hour. However, the value of having a reliable babysitter is worth every penny.

CHAPTER 21

Setting Goals and Priorities

Setting goals and priorities as a solo parent may seem like putting the logistics of life before the emotional well-being of your children. No solo parent wants to leave their children for any reason, let alone a chore. However, survival begins with properly prioritized goals. Setting goals and priorities ultimately leads to successful time management, financial stability, and less emotional stress. The lives of solo parents revolve around this trinity of successful living. Not every goal is earth-shatteringly significant and not all have to be strictly aimed at survival. If your goals are in line with your priorities and you are constantly referring to your objectives, living within the framework of even basic goal setting will move you toward larger, long-term goals. Sandi Douglas, an experienced solo parent, stated, "I need to set and tick off goals, no matter the size, to look back and realize what I have accomplished."

To make the best use of time, over time a solo parent will naturally develop their own ways of wrapping work around home life. Discipline is also key to managing home tasks that are not daily chores, yet still demand a solo parent's undivided attention. There are options to help manage these occasional tasks, but generally they all aim toward the same criteria: determine the most important household tasks, combine like activities, and assign a specific time to complete each task.

CHAPTER 22

Teaching Life Skills to Children

KEY POINTS: Solo parents begin teaching life skills to their children at a young age. It is vital that children are self-sufficient and can live a responsible life. Life skills, such as cooking, laundry, and even making their own beds, are essential to children being self-sufficient. These factors, along with the often-reported poor quality of life during times when parents are present in their lives, give us a very distinct picture of the roles that solo parents have begun preparing their children to fill as contributing members of society and society's expectations.

This need to instill responsibility through teaching life skills may explain why parents tend to begin teaching these skills at a young age. Half of the parents in two-parent homes start teaching these life skills to their children before age 9, according to a FIELD poll. However, if children have not learned the necessary life skills when they leave the home, they can easily feel overwhelmed and lost. We cannot continue to dismiss the idea of teaching children life skills for fear of losing much-needed bonding time. Are these life skills not teachings of differing kinds? Otherwise, it must be understood that life skills education is about volunteering life skills and coping abilities to employability within several different essential domains.

As a solo parent, you probably feel trapped in a never-ending cycle of inadequacy. But some sense of accomplishment is now attainable through learning life skills online, through websites for both children and families. It is easy to forget that the goal of teaching life skills is to give children skills that they can eventually use on their own. Are your children proficient in skills such as cooking, laundry, and even how to clean on their own? Ensuring that children are learning life skills will not only help them to be self-sufficient, but it will also help them to become a contributing member of society.

CHAPTER 23

Navigating Legal and Financial Matters

With regard to finances and retirement, the potential for women as a group to reach age 65 with a personal income that is 95% lower than men of the same age is striking. A non-capitalist society would take that U.S. Census Bureau statistic of 2012 and fix it. Unlike a generation ago, many mothers today work outside the home during and following divorce. For the two-thirds of custodial mothers who are awarded child support, this obligation from the other parent is a critical element of the child's survival and success; therefore, it can help pay bills and save. Life insurance on the paying spouse can also be beneficial, but it is important to remember that for all practical purposes in terms of solvency and immediate access to funds, there must be liquidity in order to address need. Finally, although retirement might appear to be a far-off, nebulous concept, it creates a financial reality as real and predictable as scheduling yard maintenance.

As with non-solo parents, it is critical that solo parents consider their estate plan, including a will, which names a guardian for minor children. With few exceptions, courts will look to the parent's will for the parent's named choice of guardian. And while, for a time, state courts seemed to be ignoring a parent's choice of guardian in a will for the child's other parent, in 2000 New York courts once again began honoring a parent's choice of guardian, at least absent evidence compelling contrary findings. As of the time of this writing, it appears that most state courts, adhering to the premise of least disruption to a child's life, defer to the parent's judgment unless there is clear evidence of the unfitness of the named individual as guardian.

CHAPTER 24

Building Resilience in Children

Being left alone by their biological fathers is considered a shock for every child. They may also feel like they are losing their connections with their parents when they sense that their parents may also become distant from them. This may lead to aggression at home or in school as they may seek attention and understanding from other people. Children are often dependent on adult protection to shield them from impacts stemming from various hazards and risks in the environment. Often times, threats may also come from within the tranquility of their home. It is hard to provide protection due to depression or when the mother herself becomes the aggressor. During such times, parents, particularly mothers, toil with the dilemma of what to prioritize: the protection of their children or the completion of their daily tasks.

No matter how strong and patient you may be as a solo parent, remember that children are just as affected, if not more so. It may take a toll on their personal development in the future. Your relationship with them, when not managed correctly, can make a massive impact on your relationship with them in adulthood. You may become more dramatic in whatever situation you may find yourself, isolate yourself from others, or perhaps even become incapacitated in taking care of your baby. Similarly, your children may also be feeling hurt, desperate, and lonely. The effects, both long and short-term, may be felt on their academic and social development. Adults may suffer from anxiety, depression, and similar conditions. A lot of neglect also arises from traumatized parents that may further result in the suffering, exploitation, and death of their children.

Effective Communication with Children

Almost all children like to hear fairy tales that have a moral basis. The fairy tales serve as a good communication medium between parent and child and also impart useful moral maxims. Children, when reprimanded for some misdemeanor, react in a variety of ways. It is not uncommon to notice children reacting negatively to such rebukes and becoming withdrawn. Here, it is very essential for the parent to realize that children do not always react to a situation as adults do and show patience at all times. Another important aspect of communicating with children is to develop an interest in their work and activities. Let the child be a priority in discussion sessions within the family. Make the child the center of all activities at home. This not only boosts self-esteem but also ingrains confidence. Avoid delegating chores to children just because they can do them. Involve them in the organization and share the workload. They will feel important and acquire new skills.

Effective communication with children manifests in many forms. As children become older, they will naturally open up to you more. They will be more likely to share information, ask questions, and express their thoughts, desires, and fears. You will find that your children will come to you with their problems of all sorts and want you more and more to listen to what they have to say. One has to take care to listen to such concerns without being too critical of the content and be ready with kind words and affectionate gestures to reassure the child and make them feel secure.

CHAPTER 26

Coping with Single Parenting Challenges

As a single parent, you may find that your problems become less dumbfounding and often more obvious. Just take a deep breath while facing the daily challenges they are experiencing, then move forward. Raising children alone while enjoying equal rights to make long-term and short-term decisions within your family requires empowerment, confidence, and persistence. At one point, all of those fade, causing you to easily feel lost and unsure about your next steps as a solo parent. For this, every solo parent should try to keep these concerns in mind. Even if they have to consider each and every one of their worries, they must realize that once they are resolved, it might not get quite as bad as they imagine. They will have a more successful family life if they think about the solutions to the struggles they are experiencing.

Considering the challenges single parents constantly face in every aspect of parenting, it can't be denied that even the most resilient of parents can easily fall into the numerous common single parent problems most one-parent families face. Life has never been easy for single parents. Regardless of how hard it is to move on and get past the struggles, they always need to find means to survive. Sometimes, it is hard to determine how they will be able to earn money to sustain their needs. They always have the fear of the unknown.

CHAPTER 27

Creating a Positive Home Environment

Have small contingency plans. In my daughter's and my case, when she's worn clothes inside out or backward, we have her select her after-school clothes the night before and ready them with at least two accessories. Rainy-day plan: Use the bathroom that the fewest number of people do, and have her eat breakfast at school. Keep in mind that creating a positive environment also includes respecting your children's possessions. Items that have no place in the open can be put under the bed, under the sink (in bathrooms), or in storage areas. Encourage your children to make their beds daily first thing in the morning; likewise, insist that they clean their personal items once every day. Ensure your home contains well-worn and well-loved communal items like books, toys, board games, and exercise equipment.

While every morning may not be the happiest in a household, you can lay the groundwork for a positive environment. One way to do this is by creating, discussing, and posting family goals. Run morning drills. With a few runs, your family's morning and evening routines may take less time and be less stressful. Hold a family meeting, with each child offering one suggestion for streamlining the evening process and one suggestion for streamlining the morning process. One result of the meeting should be everyone agreeing that clothes are picked out and school/work gear, etc., laid out the night before. The meeting should also cover the importance of using don't-rush strategies (such as finishing homework way before bedtime, using saved time to ready a backpack the night before, and doing a quick walk-through on "where's my..." in the morning) every day.

CHAPTER 28

Building Strong Relationships with Children

Inspire your child, instill a sense of confidence and self-worth in them. As a single parent, you will be the sole figure of attachment. You will have to lead the dance to ensure that your child bonds and attaches adequately. Your child's self-worth is built up from childhood through adult life. Be a good listener, compliment them from time to time. This will reassure them, keep to your promises, spend time with them, and ensure that they excel in other areas of their life. With time, children who have good parent attachment are able to build up their self-worth and will be better equipped to cope with difficult life situations.

Having a strong and harmonious relationship with your child is important. Being attuned, responsive, and sensitive to your child's needs and feelings increases the chances of closing the communication gap, having better parent-child attachment, and better adjustment. This is important as the absence of one of the parents might be seen as rejection by the parent who left for some children. Single parents must strive to minimize their child's feelings of rejection.

Quality time with your child, ensuring that they are your top priority, will help in building this relationship.

CHAPTER 29

Managing Technology and Screen Time

The amount and type of screen time used by your child may vary with age, your rules, and the repeated report of the P-word, expectations. If rules and expectations are set around screens and are continually reinforced by other caring adults, then your child will grow or not in those habits depending on the reinforcing actions they observe (or don't). Be clear on your expectations and rules regarding screen time and use of technology, at home, when visiting family and friends. This might include when they are in your or others' care. Even if your personal expectation is that your child should use technology only when needed for studies or learning, it might not end up your preference as your child grows and becomes more independent beyond age 8-9 years old. As with most things, expect an ever-evolving use of technology in your child's life as they grow and find their way in the world. Developmentally, between the ages of 18 months to 18 years, will be the greatest period of physical and hormonal growth as is the time of greatest use of tablets, computers, phones and watches in conjunction with accessing the internet.

Pull up a chair and let's talk technology and screen time. Not via screen, believe it or not, although that is how we will meet in today's digital, pandemic world. Today, we will focus on children under 18 years and technology use. Some basic, US statistics as of 2021: 4 in 5 or 87% of US teens use text or instant messaging, and nearly the same percentage of those 15-18 use social media. 95% of teens have a mobile phone. Girls are more likely to report being on their phone constantly compared to boys. Just over half say that their screen time use is just right, or about where it should be; some 31% feel they spend too much time in front of screens.

CHAPTER 30

Supporting Children's Education

Your support system should be families and friends who are also concerned with your children's growth. Your children should be in good hands when left with these individuals, and they should discipline your children as if they were their own. Strive to empower your children by encouraging their self-management when you are at work. This can be in the form of suggested reading materials, a reading corner, or a collection of science experiments that they may enjoy, even without your assistance. It is also particularly helpful to sit with your children at least once a week to help them process and synthesize the things they have learned. Initiating communication is important in helping children formulate meaningful questions, and in finding answers to these questions using their knowledge on a particular subject. Regular guided discussions can be used to assess their level of learning, and to identify areas where children may require additional aid.

Solo parents must be careful setting their expectations in terms of academic performance. Parents should be able to communicate with their children openly, in order for their children to feel understood. A good parent is able to provide a supportive environment for education that is both fun and stimulating. A good support system is also important for single parents who need to step out of the house for their full-time jobs. This requires arranging a network of dependable family members and friends who would regularly check on children throughout their day. These individuals should help tutor your children or assist with their research. They should also help make children's meals and give them rides home, if possible. Having someone to monitor your children's safety and well-being can give you peace of mind while you perform your daily duties.

CHAPTER 31

Handling Discipline and Behavior Issues

You may have at least one child in your care who often misbehaves when you ask her to do something: "clean up your toys", "come to dinner", "take a bath". What is it that you generally do in these situations? You might ignore the child because it's just too much to deal with. When you do respond, your responses are probably negative and controlling: "Jackie, stop jumping on the bed, that's not listening." These responses can cause the child to feel bad and behave even worse. Children who feel behind will be more likely to act out by yelling, ignoring, or avoiding the situation. You can work with the child to come up with a solution, but allow her to do the brainstorming. The child who came up with the problem will more likely be committed to the solution. If the child suggests something that is clearly not the best approach, follow by brainstorming yourself and suggest the other solution. In the event that no solutions appeal to both of you, simply express confidence in the child's ease to find a way. Keep it light and avoid turning it into more of a problem.

We round out our behavior series today with some general principles for handling discipline and behavior. What do you do when the child in your care misbehaves and the usual discipline strategies aren't working? Here are some ideas to help you handle those situations.

CHAPTER 32

Celebrating Achievements and Milestones

Take time to celebrate. Sure, the laundry will still be there tomorrow, but maybe not that job promotion or the amazing grade on a big test or the fact that your family recently had more "good days" than bad. Always be looking for opportunities to celebrate, creating even the smallest, simplest celebrations that bring you and the children joy. You got all the laundry washed and put away? Ice cream sundaes for dinner! Your family had an excellent week with few to no "No TV" days? Popsicles! Your youngest learned to tie shoes? Maybe just a thumbs-up or huge high-five. Former President Theodore Roosevelt famously said that comparison is the thief of joy. This concept is especially important in a single parent household. It can be easy to get caught up in comparing your life to those of others around you at work, your children's schools, and your own social life. Always remember if you do your best and focus on your own situation, that's what matters.

The most important thing you can do is to consistently celebrate milestones. Like many single parents, you might face the constant struggle of just keeping your head above water - with bills, work, your children's schedules, cleaning, and more. You may be just barely pulling it off every day, especially if you have multiple children and are splitting your time among all the duties. This can leave you feeling like you never accomplish anything. Like you never get ahead. This can easily lead to negative thoughts about you, your family, and your situation. Plus, you might begin to feel like nothing is ever "special" because you're always just running on a hamster wheel.